Monsoon Turbulence

*The world is a verse for me. It's my
soul-syrup that sweetens the pages.*

FABIYAS M V

Plum White
Press

Published by Plum White Press LLC

Copyright © 2019 by Plum White Press LLC

For information concerning reprints, email: admin@poetrynook.com

ISBN-13:   978-1-939832-14-6
ISBN-10:   1-939832-14-4
LCCN: 2019914996
BISAC: Poetry / General

Cover painting "Landscape in Stormy Weather" by Vincent van Gogh, 1885. Cover design by Frank Watson.

Published in the United States of America

For more on Plum White Press, please visit:

www.PoetryNook.com

A collection of over 300,000 classic poems in English, Chinese, Japanese, and other languages.

Free weekly poetry contests with weekly and annual prizes.

For more on Fabiyas M V, please visit his Facebook page at:

https://www.facebook.com/fabiyasmv.orumanayur

Table of Contents

The Proem

From my acquaintance with some handful of poems from the Quill of Fabiyas, I am of the firm belief that he has all the signs of a great poet. He culls his subject selectively and deals with the sensitivity and sensibility of a master craftsman. He responds to a broad spectrum of subjects that enchant the lovers of poetry across the globe. All can easily associate with his verse.

His native Kanoli Bank in Kerala and its people are seen peopling the pages of his collection of poems. This is his locale — his launch pad — from where he takes his flights into the unchartered skies and pens his perceptions beautifully well. He is like Antaeus, from the Greek Myth, who renews his strength from touch with the Mother Earth.

He wonderfully universalizes the local themes as in the "Dancing Tiger". The plight of a contemporary woman is reflected in 'The Broiler Chicken' and "The Nose-cutter". The poet explores through fantasy the beauty beyond the mystery of death in "The Eternal Voyage". There are glimpses of political and social turbulence throughout his work. The past and the present, fantasy and reality, the dark and the light, and India and abroad are perfectly synchronized in the "Monsoon Turbulence", which is a charming compilation of work from this strong signature among notable Indian English poets.

Dr N K Sharma
M Phil, Ph D, a Frostian Scholar
Formerly Head, Dept of English
MODI P G College, PATIALA (Punjab), INDIA

Monsoon Turbulence

Monsoon Turbulence

Waves leap over his roof again.
Coconut sentinels lose their heads.
His breakwater breaks, but he won't
flee to the monsoon refugee camp.

People and the press stand amid
the lightning from cameras. Their
rapture is with the waves rising
high to touch the rain clouds.

They're on a spree in the sea spray.
They're far-sighted, for they can't
see this fisherman sitting like a crow-
pheasant in the remains of his yard.

He's no pension, but only tension.
Yet he'll neither mutter nor murmur.
Now he curls as a prawn on a wet
sack inside his half-eaten hut.

If the sea doesn't swallow him tonight,
he'll wake up early, pick up his net,
and set out to catch sardine, mackerel,
pink perch, tuna and the like, for them.

A Granite Sculptor

Midday sun burns.
An iron chisel plays
sad tunes on a stone.
He enjoys prolonged
            chiseling.
The granite conceives
from his tool-point,
giving birth to a god,
who will be plagued
in a prayer hall, with
endless demands, by
someone as his spouse.
Though no narcissistic
            admiration, his
sculptures are marvelous.
Creativity is the sperm
of beauty, growing in
            mind's womb.

He lights a candle at night.
While warming his palms
over the flame, red hue
reminds him of an old
bloodshed over his god.
A sculptor is never a culprit
behind a communal clash, yet
musing moths swarm his mind.

A Hunchback Boy from Manayur

There's a miniature volcano
on his back
with mortifying eruption.
'Beauty is
in mind', his mom intones.
But nobody
recognizes. His classmates
'honor' him
with some funny sobriquets.

It resembles a cactus. He can't
eschew its
thorns. He withdraws. Solitude
is a shelter.

It's like a gas-producing
cassava; his
mind bloats with thoughts
of inferiority.

Whistles and whoops from
the playground
pain him no more. Recurrence
blunts sorrow's talon.

He falls down through
a siesta.
Posthumous pity is a wreath.

Waiting for the Shoots from the Shroud

She also dies
to be reborn in hallucination.

Her spouse's corpse
is wrapped in a white dhoti.

She makes everything
safe within the walls, slamming

the windows and doors.
Bacteria perform the post-funeral rites

before the burial.
A smoldering frankincense gulps down

the fetid smell.
She's one among the multitude who

can't see *Mangalyaan
landing on the lap of Mars.

No one can alter
the earth's flat shape in her mind.

Her peace feeds on the
scraps that a pretentious priest drops.

Her lips rain mantras,
yet shoots of life don't sprout from the shroud.

She waits
within a circle of illusion.

There's a meaning
in meaningless waiting.

Mangalyaan – *India's first Mars mission*

4

Nasik Dhol

Sound bursts from the Nasik Dhol.
Son calls it, 'Exciting!'
Dad finds it mad.

Teens are receptive to the trends of time.
Frenetic dance in the dry sand,
kindled by the cannabis and its cousins.
Dust rises from the present.
Chenda loses its human fence.

New drum shatters the eardrums.
But don't cry it's violent or wild.
To be modern,
one must hear music even in dynamite exploding,
and see beauty in a rock scattering.

Nasik Dhol *– a big drum, producing thunderous sound,*
recently introduced in the festivals in Kerala.

Chenda – *a traditional cylindrical percussion*
instrument used in the state.

Wild Elephants

Elephant caparisons none,
their enormous bodies cast black shadows.

Trunks stretch out
to pulling and plucking pleasures.

A grizzled tusker thrusts
its tusks into the mud wall of a rural shrine;

devotees drop
vacuous chants, vamoose.

People are in panic,
dash along dissimilar byways.

A young terrorist is trapped
in the tangle of mammoth legs, and trampled;

not brain, but some cruel seeds
with the Afghan patent lie scattered around his skull.

An old
bulwark is bulldozed.

A coconut leaf
is flung at electric wires; fear sparks.

The herd of havoc
uproot a banana farmer's dream's corms.

They
forage in the toxic farms.

A rusted pesticide sprayer

is flattened under the gigantic foot.

Trumpet
splinters sleep.

*Kumkis and crackers
drive the elephants away.

They will come back,
for villages grow into woods.

Inhabitants rise
as they lose habitats.

*Kumkis are used for capturing, calming and herding the wild elephants or to
lead wild elephants away in conflict situations.*

Dung Cakes

A burial
is not just a sacrament,
but she prefers cremation.

Earthly,
yet more ethereal
are the wrinkled days.

Every day she sticks
an armful of cow dung
on her wall.

She keeps a pile of dried dung cakes
(as a bouquet to death)
for her pyre.

A spark can bring out the dormant blaze.
Fire will flame over her scars, folds, streaks…
Like a pale life's splendorous end.

Will a burnt thing sprout?
But she withdraws into the thought
that everything is treasured in the soul.

Her dear ones
will find her
more lovable in the urn.

Paddling a Canoe

Their canoe zigzagged
as a snake. They enjoyed,
splashing water. They were
bold before the maelstrom.

'Those days are gone, dear.'
He whispers, and she nods.

Their canoe floats on the
silver wavelets. They stare
at a local gym's advertising
flex-board with pictures of
skinned chickens in various
poses to attract youngsters.
Libraries have turned desolate
cemeteries. Muscles of minds
decay. She reads aloud Bacon,
'Reading maketh a Full Man.'
A smile radiates his wizened
visage while paddling. Speed
and sound of new generation
boats scare them. Their canoe
shivers. Now they block their
nostrils. Fanaticism and
intolerance are more stinky
than the rotten coconut shells.
They find around muddy-red.

Brown Dog

He's a brown dog conditioned
in chains.
He lives with a castrated desire.

His urges are groomed. To be
gentle, he
must be docile. His fangs sink

into the flesh in a red China
plate. He
sucks on a daydream. Fetters

are unfastened in the dark.
Yet he
can't chase that street bitch.

There's an ID tag attached to
his neck.
Sincerity is a strain. Even a

Norway rat scratches his sleep.
He can
lunge, snarl, yap, and is proud

of his vigor. But all are transient
illusions. His
hind legs swell horribly. A vet

diagnoses an incurable fate.
Heart-worms of
despair spread in rapidly.

Master shuts gate on his face,
not paying
any gratuity. Wisdom eyes

open in his sultry brain.
Whining is

in vain before iron bars.

He deciphers nonsensical
side of
barking. Dropping past litter

in the doghouse, he limps
away through
experience like an ascetic.

Soliloquy of a Diabetic

Strolling along the tooth-track,
I lose my vibrant way in the *Black Forest.

Jackfruit flesh is tempting.
But there's a hell beyond the heaven.

I fall into the ravine of fatigue
from the crest of *Mysore Pak.

Kidneys and their cousins wilt.
Drugs devastate my inland.
Sugary desires die before my mouth.
Yet how long do I have to wait,
watching the interplanetary mission
and wondering at the Big Bang?

Black Forest – *a chocolate cake*
Mysore Pak – *an Indian sweet*

Celebrating Impulses

The huntsman's horn in
 The School Boy is non-
native. But he likes the

poem, hears a snake-
charmer's pipe vicariously,
empathizes with Blake's

boy's love of innate
freedom, and then doodles
in boredom. Next period,

he slips down from
the top of Pythagorean
theorem. He snoozes in

the Neolithic Age at noon.
His brain balks at learning.
Teachers avoid pain with

peace of passivity. Porn
virus infects his inner
system. Parents are too

busy to install anti-virus.
He draws obscene pictures
with a charcoal, as if raping

the urinal wall. He rises
up in the hashish fumes
and floats in the space.

Holes in the thought-layer are
invisible to him. He runs
wild, celebrating impulses.

An unrefined man is
a malignant growth
from the negligence.

Chemical Weapon

We're living
in a pesticide era.
Existence is in poison.

Peasants are persuaded.
Their minds are mulched
with chemical thoughts.

Vegetable gardens are gruesome.
Not green, but
a toxic shade of death dominates.

Even deep purple grapes
in the vineyards
don't tempt birds.

Nostalgic smell
of cashew blooms
steeps in *Endosulfan.

Flies aren't extinct, yet
they keep distance
from the fruit stands.

An apple a day
won't keep
the doctor away.

Chemical weapons are widely used.
Corporate target is profit.
Corpses of ethics lie scattered.

Endosulfan is a deadly insecticide.

14

Dancing Tiger

Many farms have been buried,
yet the harvest fest is dazzling.

He's one among the hundreds
of human tigers in the street.

A coat of varnish and tempera
powder conceals his skin. Pain,

paint odor, itch…he endures.
Drumbeats begin. He pounces,

shaking his hippo-belly. A
tumor also dances like death.

His fatigue and nausea vanish
in the artistic fervor. There're

hunters with bows and arrows,
dancing around him. As night

grows, waves of music abate
to end. Spectators go home

with the stars. Now he sits
in sweat under the bare sky.

Performers painted like tigers and hunters dance to the drumbeats on the fourth day of **Onam**, *an annual harvest festival of Kerala.*

My Mom and Her Home

These old stones
have undressed their
plaster-clothes. Her roof
is tattered, yet she declines my call.

Fashion and novelty
never tempt her. Her soles
sometimes soil her floor, but she
doesn't fear a stretched-out index finger.

She refuses a share
of yummy Chinese noodles
or Arabian barbecue chicken
from my kitchen beyond the fence.

She takes steamed rice
and cheap sardine curry
as five-star food to her home.
No one teases her, the ill-mannered slurps.

She hears his footsteps
from the corridor of hallucination.
Nobody chimes in, her secret whisperings.
She likes the fright, the wilderness of dark lonely nights.

Nude red stones in her wall
remain as remnants of old love.
She'll never come to stay in our new home,
she likes to be on her own always.

Lines from the Midlife

I winged with the doves
in my unbounded boyhood.
Those rainbows and the contrails
still stay in the soul.
I sweated several times
but that never lost me sleep.

Now anxieties sprout
in the sweat.
I lose me
in the parching forebodings.
Conditioned by the symptoms,
both heard and read,
I die again,
of heart attack this time.

I remember
a swarm of fireflies
decorating my dark spring.

My midlife fruits
(flowered in the torrid weather)
have ripened.
I glimpse an infinite emptiness
in the waning light.
Even the dreams transform
strangely,
sometimes with the presence
of the departed.
Something somewhere
will remain on nothing.

Dream Fragments

Opening the latch,
my mind flits out
through sleep's
window, roams
in the glimmer.

As the elephants
chase me, I dart
like a Norway rat.
My legs lose quick
pace, when mind
returns to my body.

Red tiled roof of
my old school…
a pair of eyelashes
darkened with
mascara…Sidelong
glances…
All are broken.

My dad hails, but
his words scatter
far away from my
ears. He flies in the
sky. Mind follows,
but falls upon my
body by dawn.

The moonlet falls,
its stem broken,
and the stars collide

into pieces. Soon
all disappear in
sweat, in a flash.
I drink water
from the fear-fall.

A few dreams lie
deep under like
fossils; others
vanish as butterflies.

kite

It soars
high like
thought.
A passive
thing
transforms
swiftly in
a current.
Moving
its ears as
an elephant,
it flutters
in the heart
of the void.
It becomes
unruly,
flying
beyond the
eye-limits
into ecstasy.

Indo-Pak Border

Soldiers strengthen the fence of iron wires.
Border looks like a fair face, disfigured by
smallpox. Virus is still active. Infiltrators
crawl through the mist into India's heart.
They are brave, but brainless.

A myriad of men waste their sweat in the
nearby militant camps, while wheat farms
lie locked with weeds. They harvest tears.

Machine-guns and mines can never sooth
stomachs. Both sides spend millions on
missiles, when many starve and struggle.

It's midnight, yet guns roar again, sparks
of pain fall down.

This side loathes green, and the other side,
saffron. These are everybody's colors. Alas!
Soldiers and citizens are conditioned.

I say, 'I'm Indian.' You say, 'I'm Pakistani.'
When'll we say, 'We're men?'

Stop production of widows and orphans;
invest in the infrastructure.

Remember, once we're one. We've to share
and care again. We've to barter the unwanted
with the wanted. Life rusts in revenge and rivalry.

Refugee Boat

Hatred bursts.
Village submerges in blood.
A boat floats on fear.
Voice is one among the precious possessions they lost.
Groan from the old engine continues.
A lanky lady stares at the wake through the mist.
Her memory lane is moist.

Their boat capsizes a few meters away from the new shore.
They bob on the rough waves like the wooden splinters of a society.
Some sink.
Others swim to life.

Within a wreath of strange eyes, she rocks her breathless baby gently
in her arms.
Who's insane?
That's the question.

Merchants of massacre lurk.
Another boat with the merchandise of misery will come
                                                    soon.

The Moon

Apollo 11 reshapes thousands of thoughts and beliefs
on the earth,
sprawling on the lunar lap.

I wish I could collect those pre-Apollo eyes
from the sand
and show them the moon is not God.
But they belong to
the same species living in peace of ignorance today.

Fanaticism is a fireball.
True belief illuminates like the moon.
Prayer prevents the immoral anarchy.

Not a reflection of sunlight,
it's nature's solace spreading over the wounds.

How differently it shines in science and literature!
It's as veracious as a breccia
that the moon is dusty, gritty and abrasive.
But that hare is more beautiful than the rocky truth.

The Tomb

Though building his own tomb,
he's not insane.

His violinist friend's body lies
within a glass box.
Violin tunes drizzle
over memory.
This musical funeral,
he finds charming.

A corpse and a carcass are alike
in the sand.
He wonders
how long the world has to wait
before a soul emerges
out of mystery.
Life is like a light
spreading between the two misty ends.

A lion-tailed macaque,
a Malabar pit viper,
a Carpenter ant,
a golden rain tree…
all die serenely.
But blood and brain turn
a man's death
doleful and dreadful.

Today he renovates his tomb
that stands as the sole certainty
among several uncertainties.

The Thief

They intrude even into his kitchen,
hunting.

Now they loot fruits, nuts, spices, herbs, honey-combs…
Yet he tells them about a *Black Vasa's medicinal miracle.

They come again,
strip the forest of the flora and fauna
and construct resorts and duplexes.
He's driven away like a mongoose.
On the top of a bare hill,
he hunches with an empty stomach-pot.

As he takes some rice from their sack,
they collar him
and beat him brutally,
calling THIEF!

Media cook his corpse.

Remember
he was an Adivasi,
the original inhabitant,
yet he'd to live muted in a desert
within the forest.

Black Vasa – *a medicinal plant used in the treatment of arthritis, asthma etc.*

Tughlug

You were exceptional
among the ancient Indian emperors
with vast learning,
yet your silhouette stands
under the signboard,
engraved with 'Intelligent Fool',
in the recess of history.

It was tenable
to transfer the capital
to the thorax of your empire.
But why'd you drag
the people of Delhi to Devagiri?

Your innovations turned
curses and corpses
in improper implementation.

As a ruler's thoughts
fall into the maelstrom in brain,
his subjects
sink into the fathomless suffering.

Nous deprivation determines
the decline of each reform.

It's fate
you're reborn on the earth
again and again.

A Dogmatic Grammarian

A dogmatic grammarian,
a know-all, with a frog's
face, croaks from a well.
He glowers at error-insects
with his bulging eyes.

Children gape with their
tongues stuck in rules.
Expressions hobble.
Emotions are mangled.
There's a relief in yawning.

Ma, grandma, pa and
grandpa never learned
grammar, yet their dreams,
doldrums, squabbles,
calumnies, ecstasies, and
all other throbs of life,
sounded through their
language without inhibition.

Vrishchika Wind

You were
neither a destroyer
nor a preserver
like Shelley's west wind.
You were
a native signal
to harvest the taro and tapioca.
You were
a swing for the shore,
and my soul too.

You weren't
just a parching wind
for me.
My still leaves
were energized
by your verve.

Moon shines.
Henna plant blooms.
Ghost of a love loiters
in the old melody
from a CD.
If you blow now,
a heaven will open
as in the past.

Climate has changed
like generation.
Vrishchika and the present
are passive,
poker-faced.
Season of stirring wind
is no more.
An Ockhi of havoc howls
instead.

Vrishchika – *a month in Malayalam calendar, noted for continuous wind in some parts of Kerala*

Ochkhi – *name of a cyclone*

A Coconut Tree Climber

He climbs up rhythmically
keeping his legs
within a ring of rope
like his life.

Intuition assures
the ripeness;
life-nut falls down
from the tree top.

Just a slip
will end in all end,
but practice
rarely slips.

Though the ways are hackneyed,
he's honeyed and free
under his calluses.

Morrows and yesterdays,
he never climbs upon.
He hugs today, green and yellow
like the coconut tree leaves.

E-boy

Dropping a voyage
across the printed pages,
he splashes through
the shallow WhatsApp.
Words are wearisome.
Expression seeks emojis.

Mangoes are ripe.
Song of nature flows out
of a syrinx.
Yet he kills the day
with the Angry Birds.

Ground is dry,
and in the growing shade.
Yet his foot and ball
keep aloof,
forgetting all
in the Clash of Clans.

He's the winner,
loser too,
in an endless run.
He leaves the world
for the Subway Surfers.

Only finger tips are alive.
This is an electronic growth,
devoid of the human warmth.

A Falcon, a Cobra, a Pedestrian, and Art of Death

A Falcon

> It swoops.
> Its eyes are
> a pair of
> visual images
> of wildness.
> Its micro-mind
> stretches into
> voracious rapture
> while soaring
> with its prey.

A Cobra

> It wriggles
> within the claws,
> a closed space
> for discharging
> opposite energies –
> to eat, to exist.

A Pedestrian

> The cobra slips out
> and lands on his
> shoulder. Winding,
> it bites on his neck.
> Already a half-
> carcass, it succumbs.
> Later, he too. A
> meandering death –
> from the sand
> through the air,
> then straight down
> to his neck
> out of the blue.

Art of Death

Death seems an
art in diversity.
Ultimate charm
of creation is in
its abstract end.
Many make it
awkward with
anxieties arising
from blood and
gold; a few, serene
through realization.

A Fanatic's Face

His face is ugly
as his creed,
rigid as his rituals,
and black as the dark ages
with a Paleolithic look,
but he doesn't realize.

His sneer is
a reflection of bigotry.
He slaughters smile
for being tender.
His frown is fathomless
as his fanaticism.
There's
an imminent
communal carnage
behind his buffalo visage.

Ghulam's Ghazals

Ghulam crosses the Indian border
to conquer. Bodies vanish; souls
wander in the vicarious valleys.

Fanatics essay to frighten
the music maestro, shouting
outside the auditorium.

If they sit inside, they'll return
as men. There's no discrimination
in music. Minds molt mundane

emotions, and become fresh again.
His ghazals, like AB group, accept
blood of Hindustani classical music.

Music creates blue moonlight,
when a youth enjoys black
hair-falls amidst the fragrance

of jasmine blooms. A man in
seventies skulks to1960, where
a brown girl stands half hidden

behind door. Aches and
anxieties lie vanquished
in Ghulam's voice

and variations. Men
in diverse creeds die;
human beings rise.

Mini Dubai

My town nicknamed, 'Mini Dubai', burgeoned and branched
on the bank of Kanoli canal like a tamarind seed.

Now the silvered canal sprawls on its death bed.

Busy pedestrians walk down
an ancient bridge built by the British.
As the traffic light has lost its eye balls,
a potbellied policeman dances and controls.
Jalopies groan, and modern cars whiz.
A long whistle: an ambulance with the wounded
and a van with the wedding party halt side by side
as the southern and northern hemispheres
of emotions meet at a single point.

Nostalgic smell of the canal sops in the sizzling tang from a
                                            cafeteria.

The splurging women whirl in the hurry wind among the concrete
buildings seething under the tanning rays. The stink of sweat and the
aroma of the Arabian perfumes choke the air in shops, where,
sometimes, the chicanery peeks through the glassed. The applications
drafted in blood and salt scurry to the offices nearby –only to get
the obsequies in the waste baskets. The sots creep like snakes in the
yard of Snadra Bar.

A crow sits on an electric post and watches all beneath
with a smile of wisdom

A WhatsApp Group

An island of memory forms in the
                      vast oblivion.
Emotions froth with warmth. Minds
                      are connected
through the broadband of nostalgia.
                      An everlasting
get-together of old classmates. They
                      wage war against
vices. They sob over sorrows that are
                      not theirs. Pics
of triumph get applause, while envy's
                      horn protrudes
from a pit. Origin of congratulations
                      and consolations
is from the same key. Some purloin
                      from philosophy.
One buddy's a marauder of wits. This
                      WhatsApp group is
a life jacket to escape from drowning
                      in ennui.

A Garbage Bin

Spicy smell metamorphoses
in the garbage.
The same chunk that stimulates
the taste buds
induces nausea. This is a bin
of dual relief.
As the darkness falls on the bare
reality, an arm
stretches through the hole
that nobody tries
to caulk. The stray man picks up
a gnawed chicken
leg bone, a scrap of fried mackerel,
some steamed rice
mixed with reddish yellow curry...
He recycles the
junk. Hunger can burn away
any disgust.

Kindergarten Girl

She doesn't like the garden on the wall,
where the flowers are without fragrance.
You hammer the alphabet nails into her
brain. Her little thumb and index finger
waver on a hard pencil.

She can't install her mind in the classroom
as her Barbie lies uncared at home. Your
refrains die in her ears. Her mom's lullaby
lives in her soul.

A naughty classmate pinches her. She wants
to play, 'elephant-and-mahout' with her
dad.

Your tale has a head and tail, but no soul.
An impulse-trimmer your dopey 'don't' is.
She wants to sleep in the valley beneath
the breast.

Ten to three is an inhuman schedule.
Tension termites eat each twitchy day.
Only the skeleton of infancy remains.

A nip of Salt, a Red Chili and some Mustard

Misfortunes mushrooming
from the malevolent glares
are beliefs,
as the common water hyacinth.

Eying me
drooping in dejection,
grandma takes a nip of salt,
a red chili
and some mustard,
locks her palm,
rotates her fist over my pate thrice,
and then throws the ingredients of charm
into the embers in our hearth.
I refresh, fooling myself.

A scarecrow
hanging
in front of
building construction
is another Patriot system
against the eye-missiles.
Defense is diverse.

Evil eyes thrive
from the rhizomes of envy.
They have been
on the earth
since the inception of thought.

A Red Dragonfly

I'm here in the mossy pool,
yet you never feel my presence.
I'm a clumsy wingless child.

O girl, you wear Malaysian
frocks, but I'm always naked.
You take Chinese noodles,
while I feed on insipid insects.
I cannot travel beyond the
borders of the pool. My parents
are alive away. An orphan I'm.

Time gives me wings as verse.
O lady, I know you enjoy my
red beauty, though through the
key-hole of a wedlock. I seem
not to see you watching me.
My wings give me a sense of
freedom. Now I owe all my
charms to my wings and hue.

Abu

As an Arab guest
magnetizes all eyes,
local VIPs get RIP
status. Abu sticks
his love on Arab's
forehead. Sweet
vibes waft up with
the spicy smell of
the feast. Abu plans
another plaza above
the dunes in Dubai. He
makes his daughter's
wedding unique with
the imported charm.

Currency blocks his
arteries. Love doesn't
flow. He's gifted his
wife with a desert.

Our new generation is
enchanted by Abu's
flames of splendor.
He creates a culture
of earning over learning.
Material spring will be
followed by an autumn .

An Elephant In Must

There's peril in the signage,
                    yet visitors
enjoy the turbulent black sea.
                    A benign lust
grows malignant in chains.
                    The elephant
thrusts at the ground with
                    its tusks, as
though saving itself from the
                    violent voltage
current. It hurls its trunk up
                    the sky amidst
a thunder as the loudest
                    slogan of
protest in the universe.
                    It doesn't
need a calendar. A mahout
                    can never
conceal its honeymoon season.
                    A lunatic liquid
flows down the side of its
                    head like
the lava of suppressed love.
                    Hormones of
creation are wasted in the void.

A New Species

The Thylacine, the Caspian tiger,
the Caribbean monk seal…

As these beasts disappear,
the most cruelty-vorous species appears.

They are homologous with humans
but their bearings are too brutal.

Though plenty in Asia,
their habitats are found in all the continents.

They hold the holy books
that they never read.

Tender feelings are scoped out by their tamers.
Empty sensorium.

Even the shattered body of an infant
won't wet their eyes.

They chew the cud of bloody thoughts in isolation,
entranced by a heaven.

An Everlasting Photo

An old picture appears
on the screen. Students
stare at the raw reality.
The professor praises
the photographer's
precision and perfection.
But Kevin is criticized
at the end as usual.

Kevin creates eternity,
startling the humanity.
But he forgets to save
the black girl, blinded
by a journalistic passion.
Now he smokes, sobs,
repents… for the little girl.
He bleeds from the blades.

The African girl hangs
on his heart's ridgepole.
He isn't a predator, for
he commits suicide. *The
vulture and the little girl*
 was, is, and will be a
reminder of the life lost.

Kevin Carter *is the Pulitzer Prize winning photo journalist, who committed*
suicide.

Chapatti

Her callused fingers
plow flour. A clock
pendulum annoys her.
'Anon', he's impatient

before the plate. Her
sweat creates a moon
in wheat. A soft thing
is transformed by a hot

experience. It swells
like the belly of a
pregnant lady. Kitchen
heat disfigures beauty.

Dark spots appear
slowly. Steam,
like anxieties of an
exploited wheat farmer,

rises up from the chest
of chapatti. 'Dry chapatti',
he utters his distaste. It
wets with concealed tears.

Chapatti *is a flat round South Asian bread.*

Well

A man dives to die,
And a brown frog leaps to live:
Well is well for both.

Cholesterol

A lab produces
anxieties on
large scale. A
doctor's eyes
strand on the
cholesterol
while sailing
down the lab
report. But his
words remain
unabsorbed
on her brain's
surface. Her
mind is a dead
zone of little
learning, where
cholesterol
doesn't grow.
The doctor
forbids*biriani,
ghee-rice, fried
beef, mutton
chops… A
deadpan smile
spreads on her
wizened lips.
Each forbidden
food has been
beyond her
penury since
times immemorial.

Biriani – *a South Asian dish.*

Zebra Crossing

Sweet feminine syrup oozes out.

Soon he returns to the same pale valley.
The locomotive rhythm lulls him to snooze
near the kaleidoscope-window.

He's been reinstalled on the border,
where the roar of terror never ceases,
like a statue of contradiction
with a rifle in hand
and love in heart.

Reunion is a recurring rapture.
She crosses the highway to pick him up.
What a pity!
A drunk-driver is a silhouette of death.

Lifting the latch of sleep,
he often slips out to the zebra crossing,
where she walks across with a bunch of dreams.

Date Syrup

Dark as departure
and sweet
as reunion, it's a
romantic
syrup resembling
an expat's
life. A sublime
state of
sweetness like a
wife's wait.

It's forbidden to
a diabetic
patient, but who
commits an
ecstatic sin, violating.
Rapture of
now is in a negative
impulse.

The expat squeezes
dry desert
for sweet syrup.
One sip
tempts into another.

A Coastal Myth

The clarinet waves touched the moon.

He walked like a rooster in the moonlight,

bewitched by the music and the light. The

caparisoned elephants swayed their heads

to the drumbeats. A dozen half-naked virgins

danced around a bronze devil. "Human smell!"

Everything vanished in the blackout. That

escaped fisherman appeased the dark deity…

With a wavering voice and goose-bumps,

my wizened neighbor recounts thus the

myth behind the coastal festival. I enjoy

the false beauty. There is no analyzer in

his thinking system. Superstition is highly

inflammable in his illiterate inland. Such

beliefs flourish here in the thick Fantasy

Forest, where the reason rays never fall.

Dheedhi's Daughter's House-warming

Dheedhi counts days with a sparkle in her heart.
She hopes to melt her ice-cold loneliness in the warmth of a
                                        party.
She buys a washing machine.
Pickle of mango peel, piquant beef, banana chips…
She packs all with pizzazz.

But her daughter foresees shards of shame protruding from ma's
mannerisms.
Outworn ways, the ill-mannered slurps, unrefined words…

"Tomorrow's function's limited, ma.
I'll come to pick you another day."
Deedhi's lips tremble and eyes become moist.
Several desires disappear silently in the Bermuda triangle
                                of generation gap.

Dying in a Bucket

A mere carrying never makes a mother.

A gynecologist
observes soft
feminine rhythms
on a monitor.

Currency conceals compassion.

Hospital sweeper
carries remnants
of a plastic love in
his black bucket.
His squint-eyes
are conditioned.
Pulses pause
unnoticed in the
bucket. Just two
hundred rupees
bury his conscience.
He seeks shelter in
a dark arrack bottle.

It's a cold-blooded
secret that people
seem not to see.

Abortion is an accepted murder.

Education

Education grows into a market,
where parents invest with avarice.
They want a doctor or an engineer,
not a man,
in return.

Artistic sense and athletic spirit
are asphyxiated.
Teachers are accomplices.

Children smolder.
They can't see
Robert Frost's two roads.
They learn theories,
except that of living.
Ashes of freedom and
non-sprouting knowledge
remain.

Bachelors of Frustration
multiply
in the competitive world.

There's a young soul too
among the bats
fluttering from a breadfruit tree.

Sadly,
we repeat,
'It's sad.'

English

We explore,
earn and exist
with a language
of old exploitation.

Like a mulatto,
Indian English
is a hybrid.
It's as our culture –
there's a unity
in diversity.
We winnow ideas out
of dialectal chaff.

Language
mustn't be imposed.
Linguistic
extremism is a myopia.

Wherever you grow,
your mom and hue
remain the same,
but your tongue can be
changed from the cradle.

English thrives above
creeds and colors,
connecting continents,
never demanding a passport.

In Memory of the Mahatma

Millions came like moths
from the cities and slums, and
the countryside and hillsides ,
enchanted by his bright light.

He led an army without arms
in the war against an empire,
where the sun never set.
His 'non-violence' was more
powerful than an artillery.

He taught the hungry how to
spin the threads of hope with
the spinning-wheels. Our
papas and grandpas learned
from him how to sacrifice,
slaying the selfishness.

He polished the dusty pride
and self-respect in Indian minds.

Diverse shades of simplicity were
visible on his half-naked figure.

His vibrant words caused tremor
in a distant continent too.

People adorned their affection
towards him with the adjectives
like 'Mahatma' and 'Bapu'.

Godse pierced the chest of a
nation's dream – bullets left
behind the heinous ingratitude.

Gandhi journeys through
the generations. Standing on
the pedestals, and hanging
on the nails, he proclaims
the eternal truths.

Flooding in God's Own Country

Red alert!
Anxiety level rises.
Dam shutters open.
Water wanders
among the concrete buildings,
seeking the buried backwaters, lakes, ponds, fields...

A member of the land mafia marks himself as safe
on Facebook.
Poor people are always unsafe.
They were poverty-stricken
during the steady rains.
Now they are panic-stricken.

Rocks fly down from the mountains.
River climbs up the bank.
Cries steep in the gush.
Bloated men, cattle, dogs and chickens float.

Horrible visitors take terrible pictures.
Fear fluctuates as blood pressure.

Majhi

His village
is
a plantation
of privations,
where
a variety of
sorrows grow.

Love
like corn
lives
within
a pale cover.

Pain
is buried
in the furrow
of misery.

Moneyless Majhi
plods miles
with
his stiff spouse
on his shoulder.

Here
to live
is to burn
like dried cow dung.

Kanoli Kaaka

He rolls up and
down on life's
surface as a
droplet on the
*colocasia leaf.
He never walks
with his life
hand in hand.
While heaping
up yellow metal
and rupee on the
side-walk, green
life gets wasted
in his mind's nook.
Time passes with
pastimes, but he
doesn't see.

Now his body
and arm-chair
are antique alike.
He stays afloat
like a banana
stem. He chews
bits of areca-nut
wrapped in betel,
smeared with a
nip of lime. He
spits red shapeless
fury into a brass
spittoon. His lazy
children grow up
on the mount of
money. Often
Kaaka smokes a
beedi. Curls of
futility rise up.

Colocasia is a tropical plant with its leaves having a natural ultrahydrophobic surface.

Mansourasaurus

Paleontologists collect
a lower jaw,
a skull
and ribs,
cleaving belly
of the Sahara Desert.
They provide the fossils
with flesh of fantasy.
This is
an artificial rebirth.

Mansourasaurus was
not ferocious
like a fanatic
or a rapist.
It lived
with herbivorous mind
and showed
'Might is not to fight.'
With a natural armor
of bony plates
in skin,
it traversed
the war-free world.
Mother never squirmed
under its feet.

The remains remain
with wisdom.

Mansourasaurus – *a giant dinosaur lived in the Sahara Desert.*

Memory Tonic

He takes a
tea-spoonful
of reddish tonic.
Dried stubbles
sprout within
his old skull.

Memories froth in the vast past:
his mom applies bitter neem paste
on her nipples like the inaugural
ceremony of denial on the earth.

Silhouette
of a secret
sorrow grows
against a wall.
Tear oozes out
of the past.

Memories
Froth: a baby
sucking within the
frozen arms, fumes of
mystery from the smoldering
frankincense near the grandma's
stiff body, remnants of a rape,
infiltrating fingers of a homosexual,
distilled pain from privation…

He loses
his sleep.
Even the
sweetest
memory
lands on
loss. Peace
is in the
oblivion.

63

My Illegible Handwriting

All my letters
are deformed,
beyond a cure.

Contest judges
trample over my
clumsy curvy lines.
Voice of my bruised
verse is not heard.

Sentences zigzag
with slow-moving
fingers. Unanswered
questions become
the coffin-bearers.

Ambition is lost
in the cloudy
chirography.
Black box sounds
my broken dreams.

Myanmar Massacre

Monks become monsters.
2017 is also a bloody year.

Where is Suu Kyi?
Did she lose her voice

beneath the military boots?
Paralyzed arms and legs.

Rape is a genocidal ritual.
Bloated corpses in the canal

were women in the morning.
Intensity of pain and color of blood,

the same here too.
Rohingya belong to the Homo sapiens.

Anathema rising from discontent
leaps over tolerance.

Alas!
Nobody cares shivering and shrieking.

Recurring Smell

He'd taught me
to disbelieve
ghostly things.
Skinning and chopping
superstitions,
I cooked a poem.
My thoughts grew
under his eaves.

Desolation dominates me
after his funeral.
A vague shape vanishes
from my windowpane.
A stray dog
magnifies mystery,
barking.
Being his son,
I say boldly
this is an illusion.

Can he rest in peace,
when I'm restless?
His smell
mingled with an ointment,
I often feel.
It floats
in my evening room,
giving me goose-bumps.

Gravitational pull
of a profound love
creates wonders.

Sharks

My brook has grown
into an ocean.
Pearl-spot fish
have disappeared.
Instead,
sharks skulk around.
They see
my pocket,
not my heart.
They're
democratically undemocratic.
Poetry is inedible.
Profit is
the sole default
in their thought-mechanism.

Shark morphing
petrifies me.
I wake up
from the dreamy life,
losing my serenity
in their serrated presence.
I turn
a tiny sardine,
ready to be swallowed.

Sweat

Sweat and the sea are salty
and alike.

A lazy man and a corpse
never sweat.

Mountaineers mount up the
slithery mounts.
Resistance yields, dissolving
in sweat.
Seeds sprout in the fallen beads,
life-drops.

Success floats in sweat, depositing
fresh joys.

Each victory in the history sparkles
through sweat.

The Beginning

Monsoon
begins.
The
first
shower
evokes
fragrant
vibes.
Washed
wind
cools
me
too.
Dried
soul
sprouts
again.
Fresh
shoots
appear.
Green
grows
wildly.
Like
life,
love,
wedding,
flowers...
Beginning
is
beatific
with
divine
charms.

A Monsoon Wedding

A rural priest
rolls and throws out
the wedding mantras.
The ritualistic ululation
and the music of
a toot and drum
warm the monsoon up.
The bridal garland
like a noose
awaits a bride's neck.
She bows her head
in rural Indian coyness.
Our groom learns to forget all
beside the glitz of dowry gold.

A burning wick
yields to the darkness
beyond the nuptial rhythms.
The froth of cheated love
runs down Miss Hema's chin.
She is stranded on
the bluish eternity,
along with the pressed
love in her womb.

An opened phial lies
on the floor of a hut,
showing its void up.

The Eternal Voyage

A vessel sets off from the Cape of Despair.
A brown girl of ten is the tiniest shipment.

They're fed up with the indigenous misery.
They sold everything, enchanted by the

traffickers' fake promises. Their migratory
dreams leap like the kangaroos. But Australia

is beyond the likely maelstroms and cyclones.
They conquer hunger with the dry fruits and

resist the chill with their will. Diesel and their
energy run out. They're fast asleep beneath

the blanket of fatigue. Soon they vanish within
a gigantic turbulent wave. They find another

version of the world, where there are neither
borders nor flags. They wander in the blue

woods with peeping blackbucks. Red-striped
snakes float in the fragrance of the night blooms.

Ecstasy is ejaculated. None of them feel any sense
of loss. Food is no longer a haunting thought.

They enjoy true charms in pure freedom.
Life is beautiful beyond the mystery of death.

The Fishermen

They were tossed
by starvation.
We never visited them.
Cyclone drowned many of them
in the sea current.
We were either watching TV
or playing on WhatsApp then.
We rated them low
for their sun-baked black skin,
uncouth tongue,
fish smell,
shabby shirts and lungis.

Yet they come,
hearing our shrieks.
They row more vigorously
than the flood waters.
They keep us under their wings
like a mother hen
on a lurching boat.

A Boy who Drowned

Swimming joys
drown
in the pond.
Flames chew
his flesh
along with the pyre logs.
A tear is
the liquid state
of pain.
She doesn't believe
in the ritual
of collecting ashes
and bones,
both belong to the earth.
Memory
will fill the urn.

She hears his voice
in the utmost silence.
Her son grows
in the emptiness.

Globetrotting Couple

On the Penang Island, they collect divine charms
                    that the locals see not.

While canoeing in Zambia, they fathom the depth
of harmony in the river where the elephants and
                    the hippos drink.

They find paradoxical truths on a pyramid, artificial
                    permanence and natural transience.

Even a tiny creature can create a great wonder, the
        Waitomo Glow-worm Cave shows them.

"Liberty becomes a statue in several places." He
        whispers in her ear in New York Harbor.

Black paintings of Francisco de Goya remind them
                    of some murky native nooks.

Through the wrinkled disgust, they stare at the fried
        snakes on sticks in the Chinese street.

His urge for gallivanting boils. She begins to knead
flour of next safari. They earn for each journey,
selling tea, coffee, banana fritter…They save only in
experience. Nothing will remain for their children to
inherit and to be lazy. Being on the move, this grizzled
        couple teaches us how to be in the heart of life.

Now the Northern Lights light their passion up. Like
the milkweed fluff, they fly in the air, carrying the
                    philosophical seeds.

A Cauliflower Farmer

He still stands
in the back row
with the traditional misery.

His plants
always get his carbon dioxide.
But his hope
trapped in the collapsed price
suffocates.

Farm Aid Package orbits
over his life
like a malfunctioning satellite.
His debt thrives
among the dream debris.

The farmers' dry voice flames
in the street.
He too
throws his produce.
His cauliflowers scatter
on the road
like the baton-charged protest.

The Nose-cutter

Like the rapist
and the molester,
a nose-cutter with
chilling impulses
emerges from
mind's murky nook.

He always drops
atrocities
in his wife-bin.
Male chauvinism
creates a
concentration camp
in her kitchen
and bed-room.
He's her gadget
producing
hypertension.

Her nose ring
is not
merely a metal,
but a
charm-multiplier.

Alas!
Teeth of his machete
take off the tip
of her nose,
demanding
the dowry due,
disfiguring…
Red woman sap
oozes, staining…

A Chinese Fishing Net

The Chinese Fishing Nets hanging on poles can be seen at the river banks of Kerala. These nets are lowered and laid at the bottom of the river at night, and lifted up with fishes in the morning.

Death hangs
on the poles
at our bank.
A Chinese
fishing net
sinks down
with baits
to lure into
the fate.
Doom lurks
between the
darkness and
the blue.
Joys dry in the
breathless net
at dawn. As
care snoozes,
snare catches.

On the Bamboo Raft

Like a photo
of the ancient life.

Virgin green vegetation girdles
the limpid river.

Sun shines
through the drizzle.
They're voyaging,
not to attend the wedding
of foxes.
He rows
with his eyes clung to a shoal of
fish.
His baby sleeps
in the cradle of
her hands.
Propeller motion of
his arms
is august.
This forest family emits
ebullient vibes.

They float,
self-reliant in simplicity,
under the rain clouds and rainbows,
far away from
the ostentatious pretensions
and sophisticated tensions.

Blue Whale

Blue Whale is an internet game involving a series of tasks that end in suicide, invented by Philipp Budeikin.

It appears
in Budeikin's brain.
Its baleen plates will filter
the worthless krill from society,
he envisages.
Swimming alone,
it catches teens.

It challenges Varun
in the ocean of dejection.
He takes on the tasks:
listens
to the lunatic music,
climbs
on a crane,
engraves
a red whale
on his arm
with a pair of compasses…
On the fiftieth day,
he undertakes
the last task
and falls into death
from the top of his broken psyche.

Baffling the whalers,
the blue whale swims
with its mouth open.

A Woman and her Cow

She neither worships
her cow
nor butchers it
like her fellow citizens.
It's human in hue
with innocent stripes.
She stands
in its glossy eyes.
They've been bound together
with the soul-strings.
Udder vitalizes her dreams.

Her animal's invisible sense
outdoes a Weather Radar.
Its moo rises
with the water.
A well-known clairvoyant
drowns.
Mad water gulps the shrine too.
Even the god is unsafe.

She wades vainly
through the red alert
to bring her cow
into the relief camp.

Now they float away
from the earthly stench.

The Broiler Chicken

Her comb is no longer red.
It's meaningless to preen.
She stands hunched as a deadpan mushroom.
Only flesh matters in her man-made coop.
.

She cannot forage in freedom.
She's not a living thing.
There isn't any wax to seal the pain-pores.
Bedding absorbs her vibrancy.
A dust bath, she longs for.

No cluck.
Nothing hatches.
Her thoughts transform into coral tree thorns.

Reek of feces and death dominates.
Yet her blind mates peck voraciously.

There's neither postmortem nor FIR.
This is a recurrent licensed murder.

Living Room

Our evenings have withdrawn
into a closed living room,
where we don't chat
but let a large TV cheat us.
We watch life on a screen
with a vicarious thrill.

There were children everywhere
in our ancestral home –
you could see one
even within a bamboo basket
lying upside down.
'One' is the ideal number now.
No one likes
noises annoying the living room.

We've banished our only daughter
into an adjacent study –
where she's seen
as a broiler chicken.

A savory smell,
wafting up from the kitchen,
used to tickle my nostrils,
while sitting on the veranda.
Now our cooker rarely whistles –
fast-food parcels really silence our kitchen.

Our pa and ma had defeated the hard soil –
it was their sweat drops
that soothed our stomachs.

We've discarded the defunct parents
in a dark stinking room,
even where they pray for us.

We peep into others' life
with a voyeur's eyes.

Love and fun hatch not
out of our muted words.
We aren't living here,
only imagining of living.

About the Author

Fabiyas M V is a writer from Orumanayur village in Kerala in India. He is the author of *Shelter within the Peanut Shells*, published by Red Cherry Books, India, *Kanoli Kaleidoscope*, by PunksWritePoemsPress, USA, *Eternal Fragments* by Erbacce Press, UK, and *Moonlight and Solitude* by Raspbery Books, India.

His fiction and poetry have appeared in several anthologies, magazines and journals in India, USA, UK, Australia, Canada and Nepal. The well-known Western Australian University, British Council, University of Hawaii, Rosemont College, Pear Tree Press, Poetry Nook, Forward Poetry, Off the Coast, Silver Blade, Zimbell House Publishing, Typehouse, Structo, Nous, Encircle Publications, Zoetic Press, Qommunity Media, Verbal Art, Evening Street, Malevolent Soap, Tower Poetry, Of Nepalese Clay, BFP Books, Alban Lake Publishing, The Curlew, Pendle War Poetry and Creative Writing Ink are some of his publishers.

He won many international accolades including Merseyside at War Poetry Award from Liverpool John Moores University, UK (2015), the Poetry Soup International Award, USA (2012) and Animal Poetry Prize (2012) from RSPCA (Royal Society for Prevention of Cruelties against Animals, UK). He was the finalist for Global Poetry Prize 2015, organized by the United Poets Laureate International (UPLI) in Vienna. His poems had been broadcast on All India Radio. He has been nominated for the 2019 Pushcart Prize by Poetry Nook in the USA.

He is a teacher at Gov. Higher Secondary School, Maranchery in Kerala.

His spouse is Ajina, and children are Mehna and Isha.

Email: mvfabiyas@gmail.com
Mobile: 9946657212

Made in the
USA
Middletown, DE